Wrapped In The Name

William Reader

DEDICATION

I would like to take a moment to thank God for constantly revealing Himself to me as I have seriously walked with Him in a personal intimate way for the last thirty-five years of my life. Many have had an enormous effect on my life however I want to dedicate this material to my spiritual father who went home to gather around God's thrown last year, Dr. Kenneth (Chap) P. Edwards. His great love for Jesus and the contagious manner in which that love affected him as well as all who came in contact with him has had a profound effect on me. I hope to continue discovering all that is wrapped in the name of Jesus and sharing that knowledge just as "Chap" did every day I knew him.

CONTENTS

ACKNOWLEDGMENTS

There is no way I can recognize all the people who have encouraged me over the years. To my family, friends and those who I have been fortunate enough to serve through theses thirty three years of ministry I say thank you for your support and your desire to grow with God. As you and I continue to grow together and discover the destiny that God has for us we will always be moving forward.

1 CONCEALED

Wrapped In The Name

Wrapped: engrossed in, enclosed, surrounded, concealed in
Name: a word or phrase by which a person, thing or class of things is known, called or spoken of. A word or words expressing some quality considered characteristic or descriptive of a person or thing

"A name is an individual's main identification, as well as the carrier of his reputation. In the Bible, God renamed individuals to reflect more accurately their changed lifestyles."   Kenneth W. Osbeck

I have chosen the word wrapped because during this season we are all familiar with this term. Many of us are busying ourselves with buying presents and sharing gifts for Christmas. As referenced above we see that the word wrapped has as one of its meanings concealed in and on Christmas morning we will have a wonderful time as our loved ones unwrapped presents to reveal that which has been hidden in open view under a tree, yet enclosed.

Since Jesus is the reason for the season it is appropriate for us to discover some of the things are wrapped in the name of Jesus. We will be like the little child on Christmas who opens a present and gets all giddy because they got just what they wanted, yet they cannot help but move to the next present to discover more. God has so concealed within the name of His Son so much of what we want and like the best parents in the world He has also included the things we need to sustains ourselves as well.

When I say the following, what comes to mind?

Moses:

Michael:

President:

Teacher:

Millionaire:

Doctor:

Jesus:

I would like to view the various names we will discuss in the order of the Books of the Bible. As we go we hope to discuss the significance of each name for our lives today. This is not meant to be an exhaustive writing that touches on every name of Jesus we find but just a glimpse of the things concealed in the name and a challenge to you and I to continue to discover all that God has for us as we are in Christ.

2 THE NAME IN THE OLD TESTAMENT

"her seed" (Seed of Woman)—Gen.3:15

Gen 3:15

And I will put enmity between thee and the woman, and between thy seed and her seed; it shall bruise thy head, and thou shalt bruise his heel.

This text introduces us to the fact that there is a perpetual war going on between Satan and fallen man. God here states that Satan by bruising the heel of the seed would cause suffering and problems but the Seed would strike a blow to the head of Satan and destroy the work of the Adversary. When we read this text we should leap for joy because it let's us know that though we may appear to be defeated, God has already pronounced death to our enemy.

"Abraham's Seed"—Gen.22:18
(Please See Gal.3:16)

And in thy seed shall all the nations of the earth be blessed; because thou hast obeyed my voice.

God here states that He will bless the world through the seed of Abraham. In the book of Galatians Paul identifies the seed as the person of Jesus. Blessings are to flow to the world through the seed. Because we are of faith as Abraham was of faith and we are a part of his seed, "The Seed," God will bless us so that the world can be blessed through "The Seed."

"Angel"—Gen.48:16   (Please See Gen.48:3)

The Angel which redeemed me from all evil, bless the lads; and let my name be named on them, and the name of my fathers Abraham and Isaac; and let them grow into a multitude in the midst of the earth.

God here let's us know that He is a God of personal experiences. The Angel is said to be the one who redeemed Jacob and his father as well as his grandfather. Only the Lord Jesus is able to redeem humanity. Jesus is waiting to get involved in the circumstances of our lives.

"Shiloh"—Gen.49:10

The sceptre shall not depart from Judah, nor a lawgiver from between his feet, until Shiloh come; and unto him shall the gathering of the people be

Jacob is blessing his son's and begins to bless Judah and lets him know that his seed will remain in charge until Shiloh (peace) comes. We know this to be Jesus because there is no one else to whom all people will be gathered. For us this gives us confidence in the one we know as the Prince of Peace.

Passover Lamb—Exodus 12 (Please see John 1:29)

Just as the blood of the unblemished lamb saved the people from death in Exodus so has the blood of Jesus the unblemished lamb saved all who will believe from the power, presence, and penalty of death. There always has been and always will be power in the blood of The Lamb.

Our Scapegoat—Leviticus 16:7-9

Just as the scapegoat was released so the sins of the people would not be held against them so has Jesus life been sacrificed so that we have been released. He has become our scapegoat and has been released from this world and is now seated at the right hand of The Father making intercession for us.

"Star & Sceptre"—Nu.24:17

I shall see him, but not now: I shall behold him, but not nigh: there shall come a Star out of Jacob, and a Sceptre shall rise out of Israel, and shall smite the corners of Moab, and destroy all the children of Sheth.

Balaam speaking prophetically to Balak say's he sees a Star out

of Jacob and a Sceptre out of Israel. A star is symbolic of

greatness and splendor and was always used to pronounce

great kings. A sceptre is the symbol dominion of a ruling king.

When we think of Jesus as a star and sceptre we are reminded

of all His glory, greatness, dominion and power.

"Captain of the Lords Host"—Jos.5:13-15

And he said, Nay; but as captain of the host of the LORD am I now come. And Joshua fell on his face to the earth, and did worship, and said unto him, What saith my lord unto his servant?

Here the Lord presents himself as the commander of the army

of God. In the Book of Revelation He rides as the leader of the

armies of heaven. When Joshua approaches and recognizes

who it is he falls down to worship. Angels don't receive our

worship. Because Jesus is the Captain of the Army of God we

know that the battle is not ours and that it is already won.

Because of this text I know that when things are tight God will

show up and fight my battles for me.

Kinsman Redeemer—Ruth 4

He is the one who is from within the family and willingly

purchased by paying the asking price. Just as Boaz paid the

price and then cherished and cared for all that pertained to Ruth so too has Jesus done for you and me.

"King of Glory"-Psalms 24:7-10

Lift up your heads, O ye gates; and be lifted up, ye everlasting doors; and the King of glory shall come in...

In this Psalm the psalmist introduces us to him as the reigning ruler of all glory. Since our Lord is the ruler and we are His we to are ruling in this world. In these particular verses we see that the gates and doors have to be raised because the King is so awesome that in there regular positions they would probably be messed up when the King came through. This psalm reminds me of just how big and awe inspiring God is and that I am secure because I am in Him.

"Immanuel"-Isa.7:14

"...Behold, a virgin shall conceive, and bear a son, and shall call his name Immanuel"

God had instructed Ahaz to seek a sign that the words that were spoken to him would indeed come to pass. Ahaz would not for fear of tempting the Lord. In response God gave the ultimate sign for the ages. A virgin would conceive. Not only would she conceive but she would birth **"God With Us"**, the very Messiah Himself. When I read this verse I realize there is nothing God can't do. When He speaks a thing into existence it is fixed and will definitely come too past. Why because God is with me.

"Wonderful, Counselor, The Mighty God, The Everlasting Father, The Prince of Peace"-Isa.9:6

"...and his name shall be called ..."

The name "Wonderful" helps me to see Him as someone who is absolutely marvelous. Because He is called "Wonderful" I can be simply marvelous also as one who is a disciple and destined to do great works according to the Word of God.

The name "Counselor" causes me to remember that I always have someone in my life that is willing and well able to give me the best advice possible. It is nice to know that the advice I receive comes directly from the creator of all things.

The name "Everlasting Father" denotes to us the fact that for eternity He is the chief and in charge of all things. The father in the home is the designated head of the family. Jesus is the one who has the position of chief for perpetuity.

The name "Prince of Peace" says a few things to us. The word for Prince means head person, captain, chief and the word for peace means health, prosperity, and peace. So Jesus is caring for my state of mental being, my physical well being and my financial well being.

Isa.11:10

**And in that day there shall be a root of Jesse,
which shall stand for an ensign of the people...**

The title "Root of Jesse" reminds me that God will fulfill His
word. When we look at this name we see that God has kept His
promise to keep a descendant of David on the throne. The
previous verses declare His conduct and government as well as
another one of His names, "Branch". As an ensign or banner
He will permanently be lifted up before people to draw all to
God. Since He is the root it is my responsibility to be a branch
that reaches up to Him and out to the world.

Isa.28:16

**...Behold, I lay in Zion for a foundation a stone,
a tried stone, a precious corner stone, a sure
foundation...**

Here our Lord is depicted as a tried stone, one who has
been tested I believe by the adversary and by men and
found to be not just a stone but a rare corner stone. In a
building there are certain stones that are load bearing
and without them the building will not stand. Isaiah
reminds me that Jesus is that for us.

He is also called the sure foundation. I'm glad to know that the foundation on which we rest is not on sinking sand. There is absolutely nothing iffy in our lives when we rest on Jesus.

Isa.33:22

For the Lord is our judge, the Lord is our lawgiver, the Lord is our King, he will save us.

As my judge He is the one who has the final decision on my life. Since this is the case I must do all in my power to be pleasing in His sight.

As the lawgiver He is the one who wrote the rules I am to live by. According to the Word the Lord not only wrote the Word on tablets but He also wrote His Word in our hearts. Because He is my Savior and Lord I am confident that all the laws written are for my benefit and not my detriment.

This verse also reminds us that He is our King. As King our Lord is sovereign over all things. Because He is ruler over all things I can be at peace because Jesus is mine.

Isa.41:14 & 49:7

Fear not thou worm Jacob, and ye men of Israel; I will help thee, saith the Lord, and thy redeemer, the Holy One of Israel

As my Redeemer the Lord is the one who is paying the price for getting me back to the rightful place God has intended for me. A redeemer is one who is willing to pay the designated price for something that actually belonged to them in the first place. The price to get me back was His life. He paid the price.

As the Holy One of Israel we see Him as the one who is able to protect and provide because He is unmarred and above all other God's. Only one who is holy can defeat the evil we face in this life.

Isa.42:1

Behold my servant, whom I uphold, mine elect, in whom my soul delighteth;...

As servant the delight of our Lord is to carry out the will of the

Father in meeting needs of humanity. Since our Lord is

servant of God and to man, I too must be a servant of God and

to man.

When the Lord is called mine elect it lets us know that He is the one chosen for the task of atonement. Since He has been chosen for judgment and atonement and we know how much He cares for us we are totally secure in this life.

Isa.51:9
Awake, awake, put on strength, O arm of the Lord...

The arm is limb of our bodies that we use to move our hands to grab hold of the things we seek to possess. The arm is that which carries our shield and wields our swords. Jesus is the arm of God which moves us through life and protects us as well as fights for us in battle.

Isa.53:2
For he shall grow before him as a tender plant,...

Tender plants grow silently and may at times appear to me dormant but they are to be cared for and coveted at the same time. Since He is identified as a tender plant there may be times when we fail to recognize His presence but we must covet Him because He is the answer to our problems.

Isa.55:4

Behold, I have given him for a witness to the people, a leader and commander to the people.

As a witness Jesus bore evidence for God to people even unto death. We too must be this type of witness. A witness is one who represents on behalf of another. That is what we are to do also.

Leader (King)

Commander (Lawgiver)

Jer. 23:5------Branch

Behold, the days come, saith the LORD, that I will raise unto David a righteous Branch, and a King shall reign and prosper, and shall execute judgment and justice in the earth.

As the Branch Jesus is the sprout from the seed of David who if He had not come then the leaves could not come forth. Without its branches a tree will eventually die. Without Jesus the church will be nonexistent.

Jer. 23:6-------Lord our righteousness

In his days Judah shall be saved, and Israel shall dwell safely: and this is his name whereby he shall be called, THE LORD OUR RIGHTEOUSNESS.

When I see this text it reminds me that Jesus is the one who died and because of His substitutionary act at Calvary I am now in right standing with God

Ezek 34:29-----Plant of Renown

And I will raise up for them a plant of renown, and they shall be no more consumed the hunger in the land, neither bear the shame of the heathen any more.

A Plant of Renown is someone who has been set in place for the highest recognition. Jesus has been planted by the Father to receive all the honor and we in turn are blessed because the whole world will acknowledge Him.

Dan 9:24-------Most Holy

Seventy weeks are determined upon thy people and upon thy holy city, to finish the transgression, and to make an end of sins, and to make reconciliation for iniquity, and to bring in everlasting righteousness, and to seal up the vision and prophecy, and to anoint the most Holy.

In this scripture of the end times Daniel calls Him the Most Holy. That my friend is self-explanatory.

Dan 9:25------Messiah

Know therefore and understand, that from the going forth of the commandment to restore and to build Jerusalem unto the Messiah the Prince shall be seven weeks, and threescore and two weeks: the street shall be built again, and the wall, even in troublous times.

The name Messiah means the anointed one. I'm glad that He is the anointed one, because I am in Him and therefore I am anointed.

The Bridegroom—Hosea 3

I recognize that this verse does not give a specific name however in Hosea we see one who is faithful to an adulterous wife and are reminded though we too are at times adulterous in our relationship with God, Jesus is always faithful in His relationship with us.

Mic. 5:2----Ruler of Israel

But thou, Bethlehem Ephratah, though thou be little among the thousands of Judah, yet out of thee shall he come forth unto me that is to be ruler in Israel; whose goings forth have been from of old, from everlasting.

In verse one of this chapter, the judge (one who condemns) will be smitten but in this verse God says He will send a Ruler (one who exercises dominion over all affairs) who will have permanent authority. I'm ecstatic about the fact that I am in the Ruler of the universe and He has everlasting control.

Zech. 13:1

In that day there shall be a fountain opened to the house of David and to the inhabitants of Jerusalem for sin and for uncleanness.

In order to fully understand what is transpiring here, we must read chapters 11 & 12. A fountain is a spring of water that refreshes and nourishes the thirsty. Jesus is our fountain sent by the father to refresh and nourish the hearts and lives of humanity.

Mal. 3:1---Messenger of the Covenant

Behold, I will send my messenger, and he shall prepare the way before me: and the Lord, whom ye seek, shall suddenly come to his temple, even the messenger of the covenant, whom ye delight in: behold, he shall come, saith the LORD of hosts.

Jesus as the Ambassador of the Father is the King sent into this world to fulfill the promises God made to the children of Israel and the people of faith. He is still holding the title as our mediator and fulfilling the promises every day.

Mal. 4:2

But unto you that fear my name shall the Sun of righteousness arise with healing in his wings; and ye shall go forth, and grow up as calves of the stall.

This is not a typo by the writers. The word sun here means the brilliance or brightness. Therefore when I think of Jesus as the brilliance of righteousness I am reminded of how He alone stands out above all others.

3 THE NAME IN THE NEW TESTAMENT

Matt 1:1—Jesus Christ, Son of David, Son of Abraham

The book of the generation of Jesus Christ, the son of David, the son of Abraham.

Here Matthew starts his book by identifying Him as Jesus Christ. When I hear Matthew address my Lord as Jesus Christ I am reminded of the meanings of the names separately. Jesus means savior and Christ means anointed. Therefore I am always aware of the fact that He is the only anointed savior provided that has already died and got up on my behalf. Please see verse 21 of this chapter for explanation of the name Jesus. Also look at Matt.9:27 for the Son of David. Also Matt. 16:20

Matt. 2:6--Governor

And thou Bethlehem, in the land of Judah, art not the least among the princes of Judah: for out of thee shall come a Governor that shall rule my people Israel.

When I hear Jesus called Governor it reminds me that He is in control of all the activities of God's people! This of course includes me and all my affairs.

Matt. 2:23--Nazarene

And he came and dwelt in a city called Nazareth: that it might be fulfilled which was spoken by the prophets, He shall be called a Nazarene.

When I look at this text it lets me know that Jesus was also disliked by some. In John 1:46 the question is asked whether anything good can come out of Nazareth. This lets me know that no matter how I am looked at by others, when I've been touched by the Hand of God, I am blessed regardless of what others think.

Matt 13:55—Carpenter's Son
Is not this the carpenter's son? Is not his mother called Mary? And his brethren, James, and Joses, and Simon, and Judas?

This text helps me to realize that everybody who knows me will basically look at me as nothing special. Most will never see me as anything but what they have already seen me as.

Matt 21:5--King

Tell ye the daughter of Sion, Behold, thy King cometh unto thee, meek, and sitting upon an ass, and a colt the foal of an ass.

Please see explanation for Isa.33:22

Mark 1:24—Holy One of God

Saying, Let us alone; what have we to do with thee, thou Jesus of Nazareth? art thou come to destroy us? I know thee who thou art, the Holy One of God.

When I hear Jesus being referred to as the Holy One of God I am reminded that the word holy means sacred, consecrated to, sinless, untainted by evil or sin. Since this is Jesus and I am in Him I now have the example I need in my life to live a lifestyle that is pleasing to God.

Mark 14:61-62—Son of the Blessed & Son of man

But he held his peace, and answered nothing. Again the high priest asked him, and said unto him, Art thou the Christ, the Son of the Blessed?

And Jesus said I am: and ye shall see the Son of man sitting on the right hand of power, and coming in the clouds of heaven.

Son of the Blessed is just another way they called Jesus the Son of God. By saying the Blessed it was thought that they would avoid blasphemy and cause themselves to be pleasing to God. Some theologians consider this name (Son of God) to be Jesus divine name. Son of Man is considered by some to be Jesus racial name as being a part of the human race. It reminds me that Jesus is now my representative in heaven.

Luke 1:32—Son of the Highest

He shall be great, and shall be called the Son of the Highest: and the Lord God shall give unto him the throne of his father David:

See above for Son of God.

Luke 1:35—Son of God

And the angel answered and said unto her, The Holy Ghost shall come upon thee, and the power of the Highest shall overshadow thee: therefore also that holy thing which shall be born of thee shall be called the Son of God.

See above for Son of God

Luke 1:69—Horn of Salvation

And hath raised up an horn of salvation for us in the house of his servant David;

When I see this text I am reminded that the horn represented the strength of a nation. Therefore Jesus is able to save in every area, as He is the Horn of God's salvation. Also a horn is used to call folks to meals, call men to rise up for war, caused the walls of Jericho to come down. He is still calling us to come up higher and walk with Him on a daily basis.

Luke 1:78—Dayspring

Through the tender mercy of our God; whereby the dayspring from on high hath visited us,

The term Dayspring references the start of the morning, or first light. Jesus is the start of my day. I am reminded to rise up with Him every day.

Luke 2:11—Saviour

For unto you is born this day in the city of David a Saviour, which is Christ the Lord.

The term means a deliverer. When I see the name Saviour I am reminded that Jesus is able to rescue and deliver me from every situation I face in my life and throughout eternity. One theologian says we are saved in at least 3 ways when we accept Jesus.

We are saved from the penalty of sin, from the power of sin and finally from the presence of sin.

Luke 2:25—Consolation of Israel

And, behold, there was a man in Jerusalem, whose name was Simeon; and the same man was just and devout, waiting for the consolation of Israel: and the Holy Ghost was upon him.

The name Consolation of Israel reminds us that Jesus is the comfort or one who brings peace and comfort to all

Israel. The very presence of Jesus in a person, place, or thing brings comfort to all around.

Luke 9:20—The Christ of God

He said unto them, But whom say ye that I am? Peter answering said, The Christ of God.

See Matt.1:1

Jo.1:1—The Word

In the beginning was the Word, and the Word was with God, and the Word was God.

In this text Jesus is called the Word. The Greek term used here is logos, which means something said/divine expression. Jesus is called the Word because He is the divine expression of God to this world. I am reminded that words are the means by which we communicate our wills to others. God, according to Heb.1:2 hath spoken to us by His Son in these last days. In my opinion it is wonderful that God has and still is giving us divine expressions through His Son Jesus.

Jo.1:7—The Light

The same came for a witness, to bear witness of the Light, that all men through him might believe.

The Greek word for light here means luminous/fire. Jesus is the one who fires us up and illuminates our paths as we go through the varied situations of life. It is wonderful to know that the one showing me the way is the very light of the world.

Jo.1:18—Only Begotten

No man hath seen God at any time; the only begotten Son, which is in the bosom of the Father, he hath declared him.

When we see this name for Jesus we remember that Jesus is the only one that was born into this world without the benefit of having an earthly farther. Yes, we are sons and daughters of God but each of us besides Adam (who was created by God), Eve (whom God created from the rib of Adam), and Jesus (who is the seed of the Farther) came through the seed of woman. Adam was the created son and Jesus was the only true begotten of God. Because my very existence is based on the relationship I have with the only begotten of God I know everything is perfectly fine because He has already settled the issues of my life.

Jo.1:29—Lamb of God

The next day John seeth Jesus coming unto him, and saith, Behold the Lamb of God, which taketh away the sin of the world.

Lamb points to the sacrifice since the Lamb was killed at the Passover. The Lamb is an emblem of patience, meekness and gentleness. When I think of Jesus as the Lamb I am overwhelmed by the sacrifice He made for me. He took my place so that I now have a place in heaven.

Jo.1:41—Messias

He first findeth his own brother Simon, and saith unto him, We have found the Messias, which is, being interpreted, the Christ.

Messias means Christ and we have already discussed this name.

Jo.1:49—Rabbi, Son of God, King of Israel

Nathanael answered and saith unto him, Rabbi, thou art the Son of God; thou art the King of Israel.

Rabbi means Master, which is a title of honor. (See verse 38 of this chapter)

Son of God is representative of His personal identity.

King of Israel is representative of His official identity as the real descendant of David. Do remember that where a king lives is the foundation of power in a nation. As King of my life Jesus is the foundation of all power and authority in my life.

John 6:35 & 48—Bread of Life (Do check out verse 51)

And Jesus said unto them, I am the bread of life: he that cometh to me shall never hunger; and he that believeth on me shall never thirst.

When I hear Jesus identifying Himself as the bread of life I am reminded that bread is the thing that can sustain and nourish me. The thing about bread is that it looks good and smells good but to really enjoy the essence of bread one must eat it. If we are to get the full benefit of life in Christ it is not enough to see Jesus in the world, know he is real or to smell the aroma of His goodness. We must taste (take Him in) to fully experience real

Life in Christ.

John 8:58—I Am
Jesus said unto them, Verily, verily, I say unto you, Before Abraham was, I am.

Some may say this is not a name as it is used here because what Jesus was actually saying is this: Before Abraham was born I existed. Jesus basically let's everyone know that we can't phantom a time when He did not exist. Whenever I here "I Am" it reminds me that God is everything I need to make it in this life.

John 10:9—The Door

I am the door: by me if any man enter in, he shall be saved, and shall go in and out, and find pasture.

The word door means portal, entrance, or gate. Therefore if I follow the instructions He who is the way gives I will find a place of rest, refreshing and nourishment.

John 10:11 & 14—Good Shepherd
I am the good shepherd: the good shepherd giveth his life for the sheep.

When I think of the name Good Shepherd I am reminded that the shepherd is assigned the task of caring for every aspect of the sheep's lives. He protects, provides and prepares for every contingency in the life of His sheep. I'm glad the Lord is my shepherd.

John 11:25—Resurrection & Life

What I hear Jesus saying to the sister's and all who hear is this: Don't you understand that I am the only one here who has the power to raise your brother. I don't have to wait I can do it right now. He alone has the power over death therefore He alone has the power to raise the dead. When things appear to have no vitality in my life I am confident that He who has risen from the grave can bring life to my circumstances

John 14:6—Way, Truth, and Life

I believe this is self-explanatory.

John 15:1—The Vine

When I here Jesus referred to as the vine it reminds me that what I become is directly linked to the Him because the vine determines how great the grapes really are.

John 19:19—King of Jews

And Pilate wrote a title, and put it on the cross. And the writing was, JESUS OF NAZARETH THE KING OF THE JEWS.

Self-explanatory

Acts:

2:27 & 3:14—Holy One

3:15—Prince of Life

4:27—Holy Child

5:31—Prince

7:59—Lord Jesus

7:52 & 22:14—Just One

10:36—Lord of All

11:17—Lord Jesus Christ

Romans

3:24—Christ Jesus

15:12—Root of Jesse

Corinthians

I Cor.1:2 & 30—Christ Jesus

1 Cor. 1:24—Power of God & Wisdom of God

But unto them which are called, both Jews and Greeks, Christ the power of God, and the wisdom of God.

When I see Jesus referred to as the Power of God here I am reminded that the word for power here is dunamis. In the Greek the word means miraculous power. Therefore I personally get excited because the miraculous power of God is dwelling on the inside of me at all times. At any given moment when situations are not in my favor all I need to remember is that "greater is he that is in me than he that is in the world."

When I realize that Jesus is the wisdom of God and I understand wisdom to be the ability to judge correctly and follow the correct course of action. John quotes Jesus as being "the way, the truth, and the life." When we have Jesus inside we have access to the correct response in every situation. I personally believe that we

WRAPPED IN THE NAME

have spiritual discernment and common sense all
wrapped in one package. (Jesus)

1 Cor 5:7—Our Passover

**Purge out therefore the old leaven, that ye may
be a new lump, as ye are unleavened. For even
Christ our passover is sacrificed for us:**

We know that the Passover is the time that the Jewish
people celebrated the day that God caused death to go
around those who had marked their houses with blood
on the doorpost, thereby initiating there release from
bondage in Egypt. As I remember Jesus is my Passover
I realize that Jesus has released me from the power,
penalty, and presence of sin. I'm free because He
passed through.

1 Cor. 15:45 & 47—Second Adam & Second Man

**And so it is written, The first man Adam was
made a living soul; the last Adam was made a
quickening spirit. The first man is of the earth,
earthy: the second man is the Lord from
heaven.**

Just as Adam was representative of all humanity and in
him all have sinned and are separated from God, so too
does Jesus represents all humanity and in Him all
humanity is given an opportunity to spend eternity with
God. Remember all people have a choice to make
because Jesus died and got up.

II Cor.4:4—Image of God

Eph 2:20—Chief Corner Stone
And are built upon the foundation of the apostles and prophets, Jesus Christ himself being the chief corner stone;

During this time when a building was erected there where stones laid at each corner which were larger than the others. These were called corner stones and if they were not in place the whole structure was faulty. Since Jesus is our chief corner stone the essence of our being as Christians is built upon Him and Him alone. If He doesn't occupy the proper place in our lives we are subject to crumble at any time.

Eph 5:23—Head of the Church
For the husband is the head of the wife, even as Christ is the head of the church: and he is the saviour of the body.

The "Head" is the person with the designated right to direct and be in charge. Jesus is the one with the designated authority in the church. As the "Head" he is also given the responsibility of protecting, providing, and preparing His church at all times.

Name above All Names—Phil.2:9

That is self explanatory.

Col 1:15—First-Born of every Creature
Who is the image of the invisible God, the firstborn of every creature:

The Firstborn are the ones with special privileges. They receive a double portion of inheritance, they are the ones 1st in succession for the estate, they are also the ones who are the officiating High Priest in a household. The firstborn also assume the role of "Headship" at the demise of the "Head". I'm glad the "Firstborn" of the church will never ever die and will always act as "Head" in all my affairs.

1 Tim 2:5—Mediator

For there is one God, and one mediator between God and men, the man Christ Jesus;

The word mediator means go-between, middle person, one whose office it is to reconcile two people, a peacemaker. Jesus is all of this to me, for if I had to stand before God without my mediator I would surely be sentenced to eternity in hell.

1 Tim 2:6—Ransom
Who gave himself a ransom for all, to be testified in due time.

Ransom is that thing which allows for captives to be redeemed by paying the price required. He exchanged

Himself for me so that I could be made free. True the price was high but Jesus paid it all just for me.

1 Tim 6:15—Potentate, King of Kings, Lord of Lords

Which in his times he shall shew, who is the blessed and only Potentate, the King of kings, and Lord of lords;

King of Kings and Lord of Lords are self explanatory. The word "Potentate" is spelled dunastees in the Greek and it means one who is mighty. In the text Jesus is called the blessed and only mighty one. He is the ruler of the universe and in the eyes of the Father and me He is the one and only ruler of the universe.

Titus 2:13—The Blessed Hope

Heb 1:2—Heir of all Things

Hath in these last days spoken unto us by his Son, whom he hath appointed heir of all things, by whom also he made the worlds;

The word heir means one who acquires anything by inheritance. God owns all things and the Bible says that Jesus is the receiver of all things belonging to God. Because I am in Christ and a joint-heir I receive all through Jesus.

Heb 2:10—Captain of Salvation

For it became him, for whom are all things, and by whom are all things, in bringing many sons unto glory, to make the captain of their salvation perfect through sufferings.

The word captain here means leader. Therefore when I think of Jesus as Captain of my Salvation I see him as the one in charge of my salvation because He paid for it with His blood.

Heb 3:1—Apostle & High Priest

Wherefore, holy brethren, partakers of the heavenly calling, consider the Apostle and High Priest of our profession, Christ Jesus;

Apostle is one who is sent. The High Priest is the person who pleads the cause of the people before God.

As my Apostle Jesus is the messenger sent from God to plead my cause to God.

Heb 5:9—Author of Salvation

And being made perfect, he became the author of eternal salvation unto all them that obey him;

The word author in the Greek is "aitios" and it means cause. Simply put Jesus is the reason I am able to have salvation.

Heb 6:20—Forerunner

Whither the forerunner is for us entered, even Jesus, made an high priest for ever after the order of Melchisedec.

The word forerunner in the Greek is "prodromos" and it means one who goes before others to prepare the way. He is the one who does it first. The scout's in the westerns always mapped out the path by traveling it first. Jesus has already made the way and He is yet continuing to make a way for us in earth and heaven.

Heb 7:22—Surety
By so much was Jesus made a surety of a better testament.

The word surety in the Greek is "enguos" and it means to pledge ones name, property or influence that a certain thing will be done. Jesus has pledged His name so we could enter into the new covenant of grace with God. We find ourselves in an awesome position when we realize that Jesus is backing us before the father.

Heb 12:2—Author and Finisher of our Faith

Looking unto Jesus the author and finisher of our faith; who for the joy that was set before him endured the cross, despising the shame, and is set down at the right hand of the throne of God.

The word author in the Greek is "archeegon" and it means Prince-Leader, Captain, Originator, and the word finisher in the Greek is "teleioteen" and it means perfector. It is important to note that the word our, is not in the original text, therefore Jesus is the author and finisher of faith. To put it in my terms He is the beginning and end of faith. If I put my faith in anyone or thing other than Jesus I will fall because He is the only one who can ignite faith and perfect that which He has ignited.

1 Peter 2:6-8—Stone of Stumbling; Rock of Offence

Wherefore also it is contained in the scripture, Behold, I lay in Sion a chief corner stone, elect, precious: and he that believeth on him shall not be confounded.

Unto you therefore which believe he is precious: but unto them which be disobedient,

the stone which the builders disallowed, the same is made the head of the corner,

And a stone of stumbling, and a rock of offence, even to them which stumble at the word, being disobedient: whereunto also they were appointed.

Although verses 6-7 do contain names of Jesus we will discuss the two names in verse 8 since the others have already been addressed elsewhere. When we look at these two names we should actually think the same thing because they basically mean the same thing. Stone of Stumbling means the cause for suffering and falling, while Rock of Offence means a snare one stumbles against. Jesus becomes a Stone of Stumbling and a Rock of Offence to those who don't believe and precious to those of us who do.

1 Peter 2:25—Shepherd & Bishop of Souls

For ye were as sheep going astray; but are now returned unto the Shepherd and Bishop of your souls.

A shepherd is the one who protects, provides, leads, restores and generally cares for the sheep. The Bishop is charged with the oversight, inspection and the task of watching over our interest. The Bishop is the guardian of the people. The psalmist said it best when he said "The Lord is my shepherd". All I can say is watch over me Lord.

1 John 2:1—Advocate

My little children, these things write I unto you, that ye sin not. And if any man sin, we have an advocate with the Father, Jesus Christ the righteous:

In the Greek the word advocate is "parakleeton" which is the same word used for the Holy Spirit in other parts of scripture, which generally means comforter. The extended meaning here is one summoned alongside, especially to serve as a helper. The advocate is called alongside to plead the cause of one person before another. Jesus has been summoned by God to come alongside us to plead our cause. I'm glad I don't have to stand on my own merit and plead my innocence before God or man all I have to do is rest on the merit of Jesus.

Rev 1:5—First Begotten of the Dead

And from Jesus Christ, who is the faithful witness, and the first begotten of the dead, and the prince of the kings of the earth. Unto him that loved us, and washed us from our sins in his own blood,

The Greek word used here is "prototokos" and it denotes the first to do a thing. I like what one commentator said when he explained this verse this way. Jesus is the first to rise and not die again. If we think about anyone else who rose from the dead we must admit that they died again. Though I may die I am assured to rise again and live forever because Jesus already did it and promised us that we could live with Him.

Rev 1:8—Alpha & Omega

I am Alpha and Omega, the beginning and the ending, saith the Lord, which is, and which was, and which is to come, the Almighty.

The words alpha and omega, are the first and last letters of the Greek alphabets. When you said this to the Jewish people of this time they understood it to mean the whole thing from beginning to end. Jesus is saying to us that He truly is all that we need from start to finish.

Rev 1:17—First & Last

And when I saw him, I fell at his feet as dead. And he laid his right hand upon me, saying unto me, Fear not; I am the first and the last:

At a glance this name means the same thing as the one previous to it. This would not be untrue. One commentator said Jesus is saying here that He is first because there was no God before Him and last because there is no other after Him. Jamieson, Faulk & Brown in their commentary say that He is first because all things flow from Him and last because all things return to Him.

Rev 3:14—Amen, Beginning of creation of God

And unto the angel of the church of the Laodiceans write; These things saith the Amen, the faithful and true witness, the beginning of the creation of God;

The word "amen" means true, certain, and faithful. When Jesus says He is the "Amen" I realize that I can count on what He says because He is totally reliable.

When I hear Him being referred to as the "beginning of the creation of God" I don't see Him as the one created first but as the originator of all creation. He started it all.

Rev 5:5—Lion of Judah

And one of the elders saith unto me, Weep not: behold, the Lion of the tribe of Juda, the Root of David, hath prevailed to open the book, and to loose the seven seals thereof.

The lion is the king of the animal world. When we see a lion we think of authority. Lion's were generally used in the word to denote strength, boldness, and ferocity. Judah is the tribe of praise. When I see the name "Lion of the Tribe of Judah" I focus on the strength and authority of praise in heaven. I am reminded to praise in all things for God takes up residence in my praise and begins to move on my behalf.

Rev 5:6—Lamb

And I beheld, and, lo, in the midst of the throne and of the four beasts, and in the midst of the elders, stood a Lamb as it had been slain, having seven horns and seven eyes, which are the seven Spirits of God sent forth into all the earth.

The "Lamb" in scripture and our society is a symbol of innocence and humility. The "Lamb" was also an instrument commonly offered in sacrificial services. Jesus as my "Lamb" has become the sacrifice to allow me to freely get in the presence of God.

Rev 19:13—Word of God

And he was clothed with a vesture dipped in blood: and his name is called The Word of God.

I believe that this is self-explanatory. However I do want to point out that this name is unique to Jesus.

Rev 22:16—Morning Star

I Jesus have sent mine angel to testify unto you these things in the churches. I am the root and the offspring of David, and the bright and morning star.

The "morning star" is a star that during some seasons of the year precedes the rising of the sun and leads on the day. It is considered the most beautiful of stars because of the way the sunlight reflects colors off it as it rises. The "morning star" is the first thing at the dawn of the day. Since Jesus is the "Morning Star" I view Him as the one who leads my day and the very first thing I focus on at the dawn of any new day.

4 WHAT DID JESUS SAY

John 4:25-26—Messiah

The woman saith unto him, I know that Messias cometh, which is called Christ: when he is come, he will tell us all things. Jesus saith unto her, I that speak unto thee am he.

Jesus says to the woman I am the anointed one and I can share all things with you right now. There is thus no need for me to wait for my change, I can go to Him and expect a response for the questions of life

John 5:22—The Judge

For the Father judgeth no man, but hath committed all judgment unto the Son:

Jesus has been given the final say in all areas. As I walk with Him on a daily basis my final judgment is made secure

JOHN 6:35 –Bread of Life
And Jesus said unto them, I am the bread of life: he that cometh to me shall never hunger; and he that believeth on me shall never thirst.

When I think of Jesus as being the bread of life I am reminded that He then is my permanent provision and my needs are all encompassed in Jesus

John 8:12—Light of The World

Then spake Jesus again unto them, saying, I am the light of the world: he that followeth me shall not walk in darkness, but shall have the light of life.

As I read this joy floods my heart because darkness cannot occupy a territory when light is present. Light is also used to show us our way when we are at times lost. Jesus is my guide and my protector as He is the light of the world.

John 10:10-11—The Good Shepherd

The thief cometh not, but for to steal, and to kill, and to destroy: I am come that they might have life, and that they might have it more abundantly.

I am the good shepherd: the good shepherd giveth his life for the sheep.

Remember a shepherd is charged with caring for the sheep. When sheep have a good shepherd their lives are easy. My life has been and will be made easy because of Jesus

John 10:36—Son of God

Say ye of him, whom the Father hath sanctified, and sent into the world, Thou blasphemest; because I said, I am the Son of God?

John 16:33—World Overcomer

These things I have spoken unto you, that in me ye might have peace. In the world ye shall have

tribulation: but be of good cheer; I have overcome the world.

I am excited because I am in Christ and He has already overcome the world, thus the difficulties of this world cannot over take me because he has already triumphed over the world.

John 11:25—Resurrection and Life

Jesus said unto her, I am the resurrection, and the life: he that believeth in me, though he were dead, yet shall he live:

Jesus here boldly proclaims that He and He alone can give, sustain, resurrect and restore life. No matter how down things may appear, Jesus has the last say and my life is in His hands.

John 14:6—Way, Truth, And Life

Jesus saith unto him, I am the way, the truth, and the life: no man cometh unto the Father, but by me.

The only way to get to God is to come through Jesus. Many may try other means but I have decided to follow Jesus.

John 15:5—The Vine

I am the vine, ye are the branches: He that abideth in me, and I in him, the same bringeth forth much fruit: for without me ye can do nothing.

As the vine Jesus provides my substance for life. If the branch becomes disconnected from the vine it will not be able to produce fruit and eventually dry up and die. I must remain connected to Jesus so that I too can produce much fruit. My work cannot be done nor my destiny fulfilled if I break away from the vine.

John 17:1-2—Has All Power

These words spake Jesus, and lifted up his eyes to heaven, and said, Father, the hour is come; glorify thy Son, that thy Son also may glorify thee:

As thou hast given him power over all flesh, that he should give eternal life to as many as thou hast given him.

He has all the power so I think it is in my best interest to stay with Jesus. Any smart person would chose to continue to abide with the one who has all power.

John 18:36-37—A King

Jesus answered, My kingdom is not of this world: if my kingdom were of this world, then would my servants fight, that I should not be delivered to the Jews: but now is my kingdom not from hence.

Pilate therefore said unto him, Art thou a king then? Jesus answered, Thou sayest that I am a king. To this end was I born, and for this cause came I into the world, that I should bear witness unto the truth. Every one that is of the truth heareth my voice.

Jesus has dominion over all things, I surrender to the King.

At the beginning of this journey we mentioned that one of the meanings of the word wrapped was "concealed in." I realize that this may not be the most exhaustive or the most theologically deep list that one could compile. Yet when we review the names mentioned we realize that there is a lot concealed in the name of Jesus. HE TRULY IS ALL THAT!

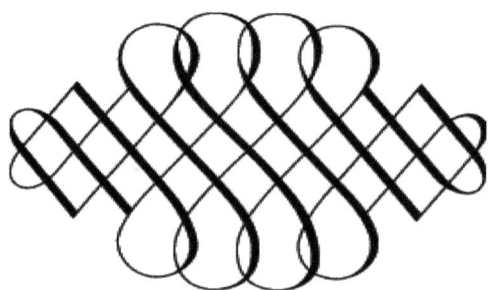

ABOUT THE AUTHOR

William Reader, a pastor, trainer, human behavior consultant, life coach, dream coach and relationship coach has been in service to others for over thirty years. He has traveled far and wide sharing his love for God and others. His belief that God has great things in store for all of us has been the focus in all he has done. His life purpose is to help people make the crooked ways straight in their lives.